LABELING ANIMAL AND PLANT CELLS

AN ADVANCED ANATOMY
FOR KIDS WORKBOOK GRADE 6

Children's Anatomy Books

BABY PROFESSOR
EDUCATION KIDS

Speedy Publishing LLC
40 E. Main St. #1156
Newark, DE 19711
www.speedypublishing.com

LEARNING IS FUN!

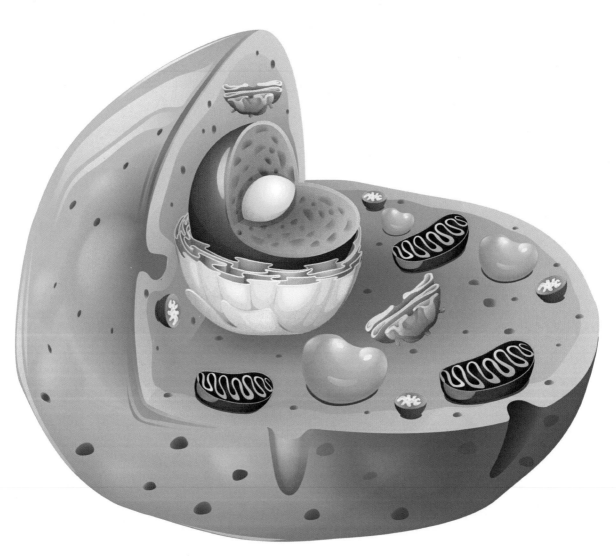

animal cell

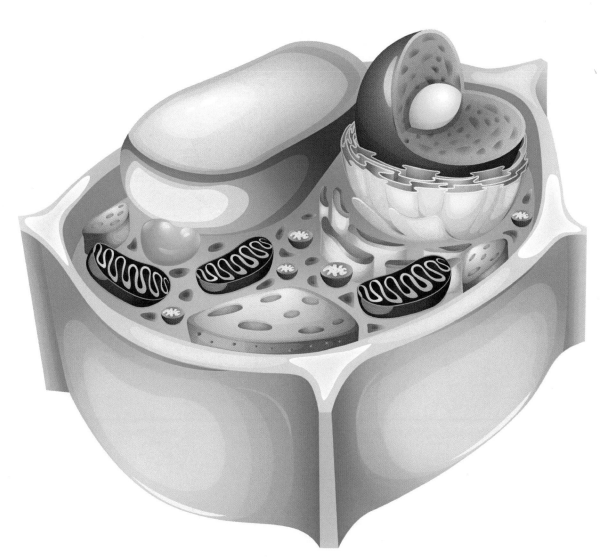

plant cell

LET US LOOK AT...

PLANT CELLS

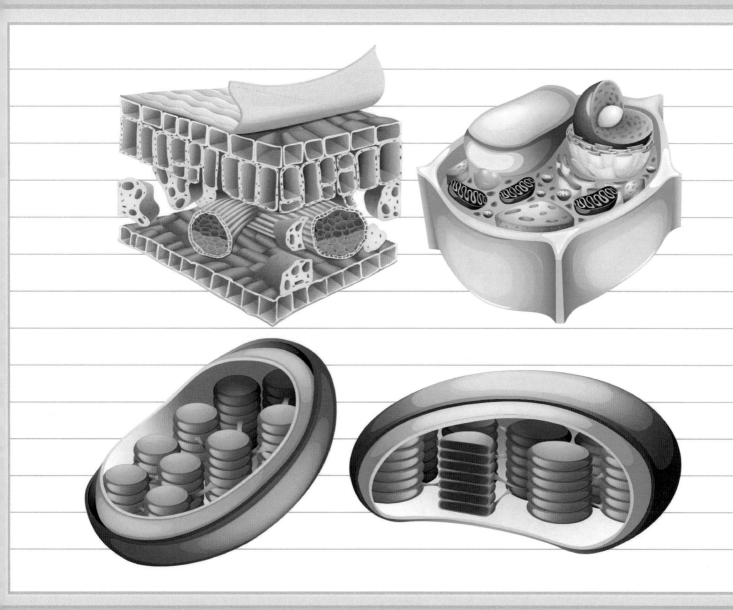

LEAF ANATOMY

AND IT'S STRUCTURE

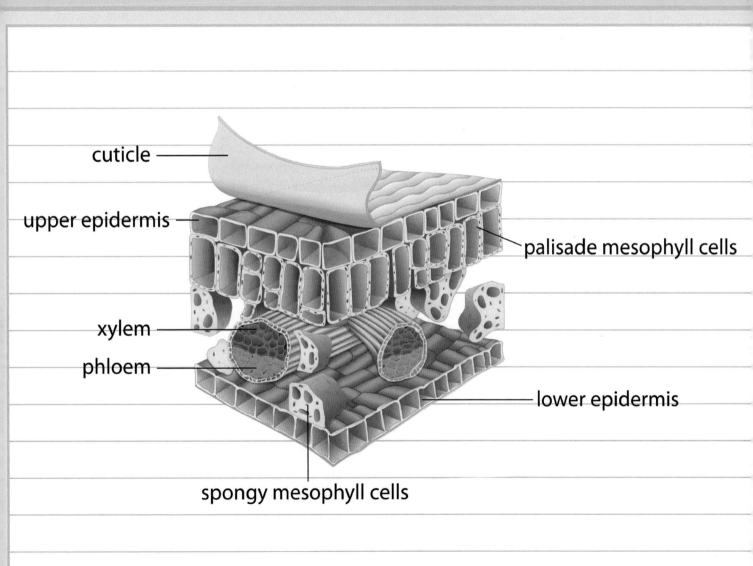

cuticle

upper epidermis

palisade mesophyll cells

xylem

phloem

lower epidermis

spongy mesophyll cells

PLANT CELL ANATOMY

AND IT'S STRUCTURE

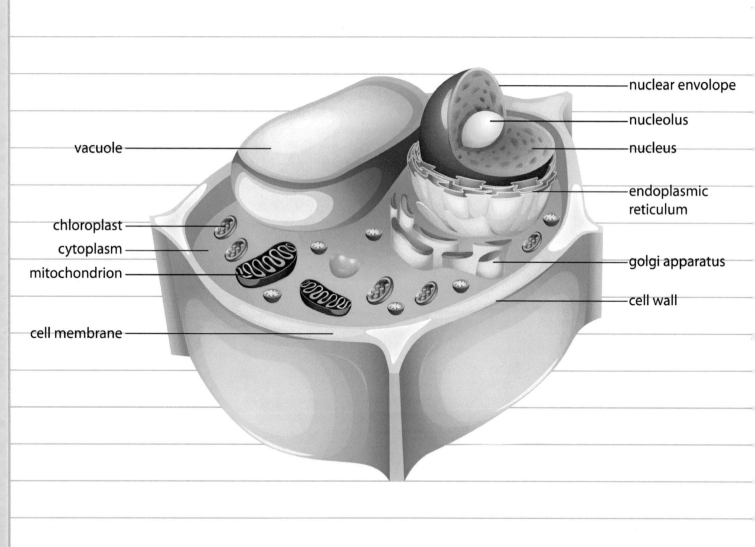

nuclear envolope

nucleolus

nucleus

endoplasmic reticulum

vacuole

golgi apparatus

chloroplast

cytoplasm

mitochondrion

cell wall

cell membrane

CHLOROPLAST ANATOMY

CHLOROPLAST STRUCTURE

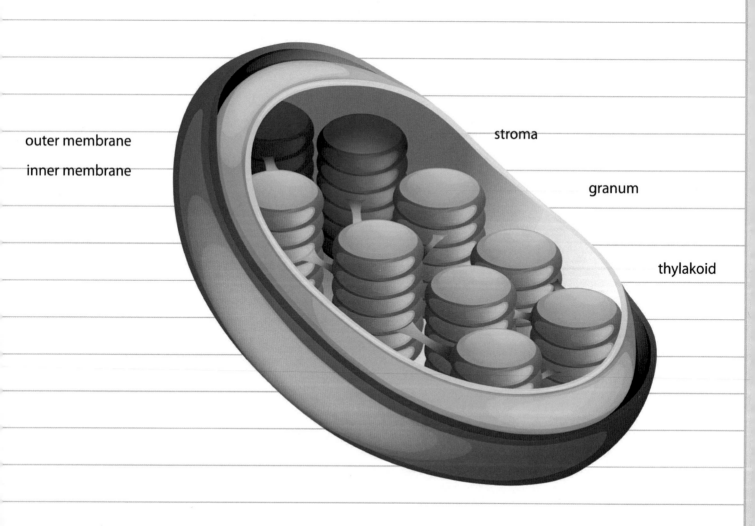

outer membrane

inner membrane

stroma

granum

thylakoid

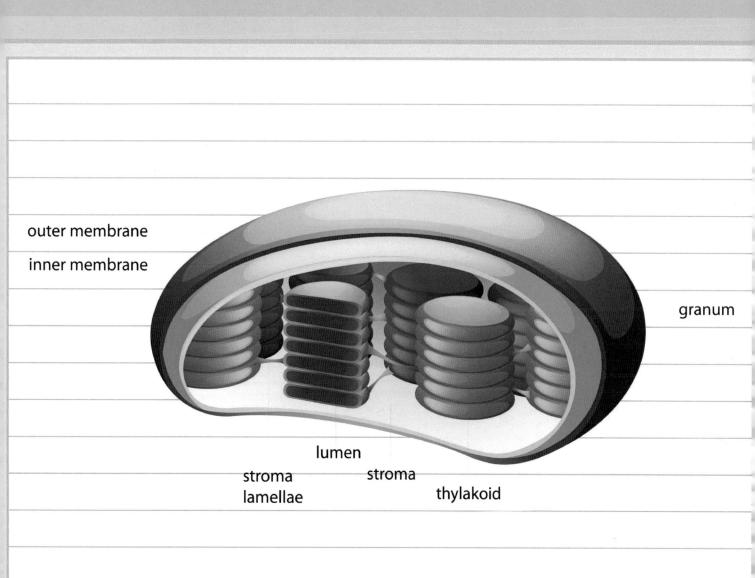

outer membrane

inner membrane

granum

lumen

stroma

stroma

lamellae

thylakoid

CHLOROPLAST STRUCTURE

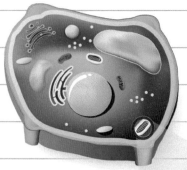

Plant cell

Chloroplast

Granum

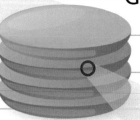

Thylakoid

Thylakoid lumen

PROCESS OF PHOTOSYNTHESIS

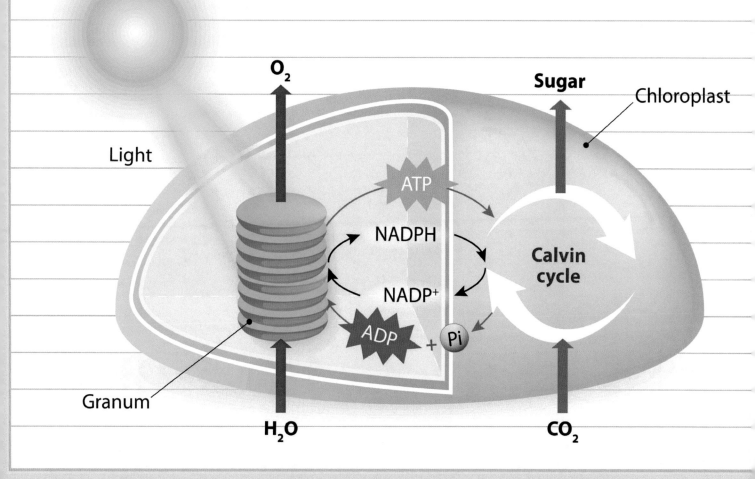

LEAF ANATOMY & PHOTOSYNTHESIS

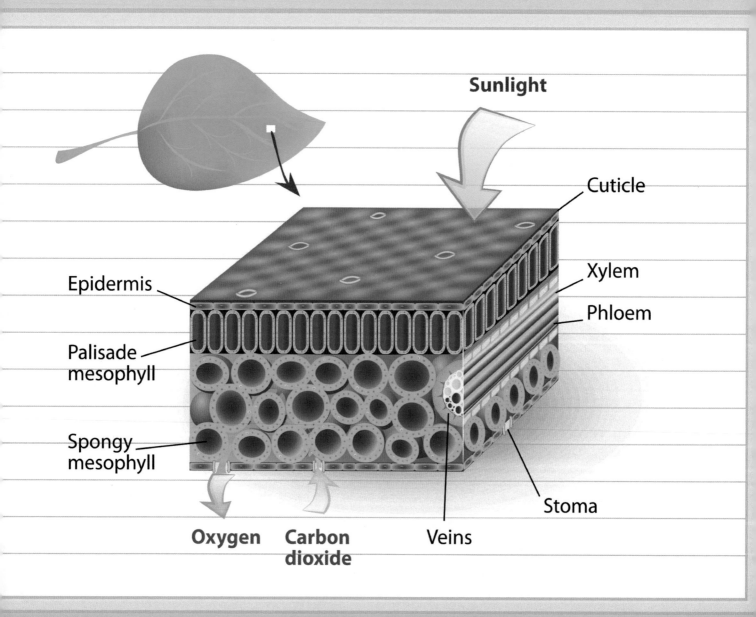

Sunlight

Cuticle

Xylem

Phloem

Epidermis

Palisade mesophyll

Spongy mesophyll

Oxygen

Carbon dioxide

Veins

Stoma

LIGHT REACTION & CALVIN CYCLE

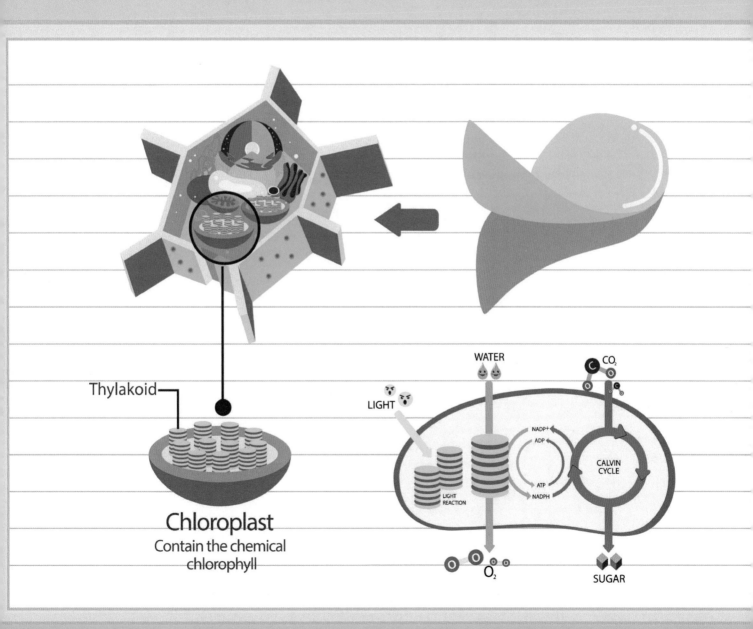

Thylakoid

Chloroplast
Contain the chemical chlorophyll

WATER

CO$_2$

LIGHT

NADP+

ADP

ATP

NADPH

LIGHT REACTION

CALVIN CYCLE

O$_2$

SUGAR

PLANT GUARD CELL & STOMA

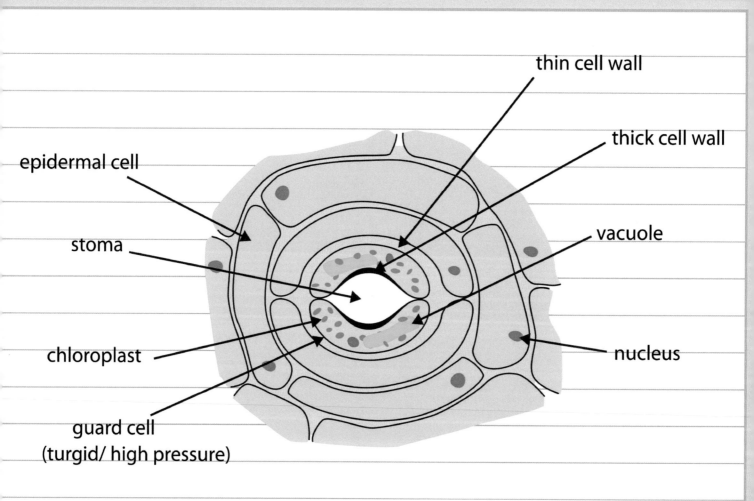

thin cell wall

thick cell wall

epidermal cell

vacuole

stoma

chloroplast

nucleus

guard cell
(turgid/ high pressure)

Stoma Open

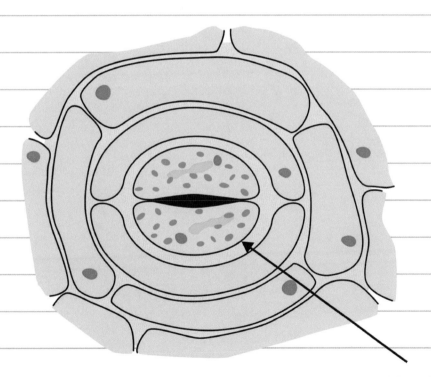

guard cell
(flaccid/low pressure)

Stoma Closed

PLANT CELL COMPONENTS

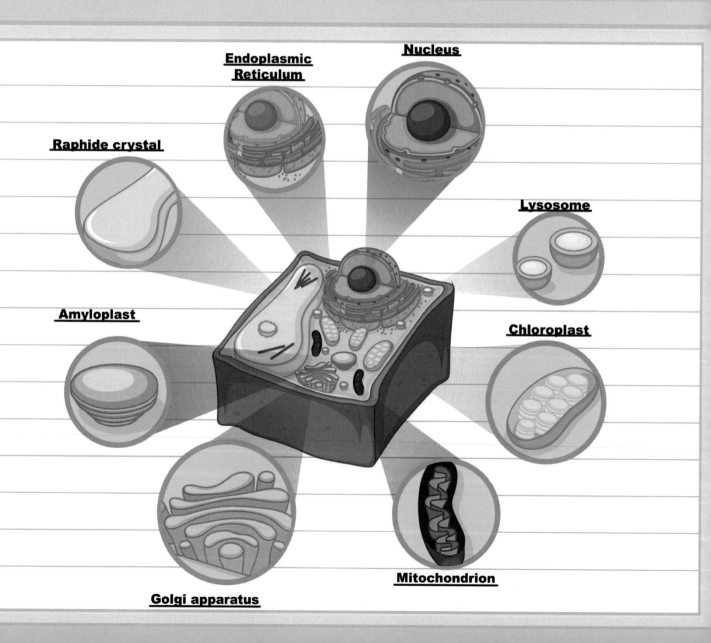

GOLGI APPARATUS

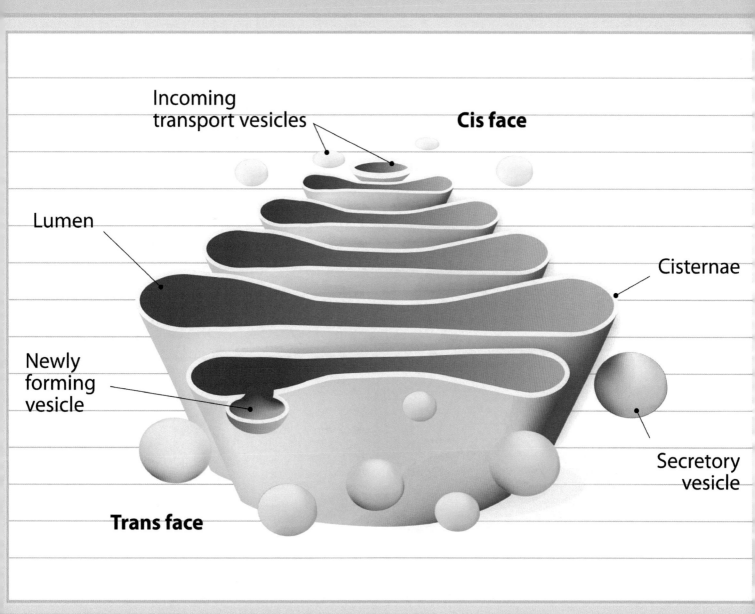

Incoming transport vesicles

Cis face

Lumen

Cisternae

Newly forming vesicle

Secretory vesicle

Trans face

ENDOPLASMIC RETICULUM

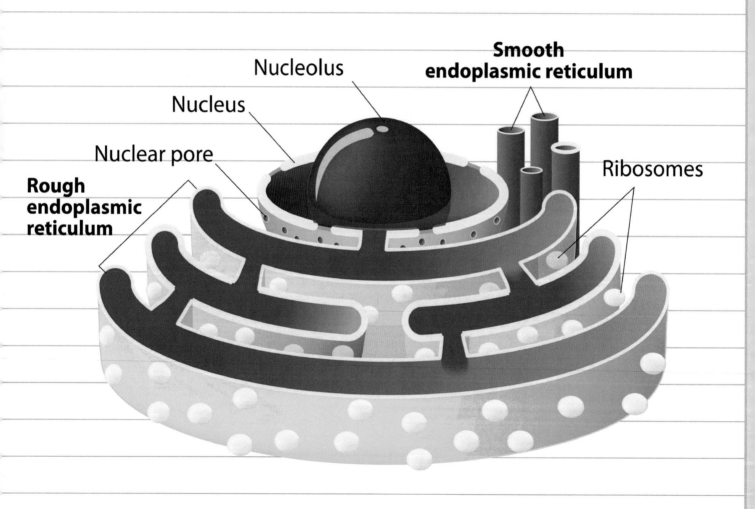

Nucleolus

Nucleus

Nuclear pore

Smooth endoplasmic reticulum

Rough endoplasmic reticulum

Ribosomes

MITOCHONDRION

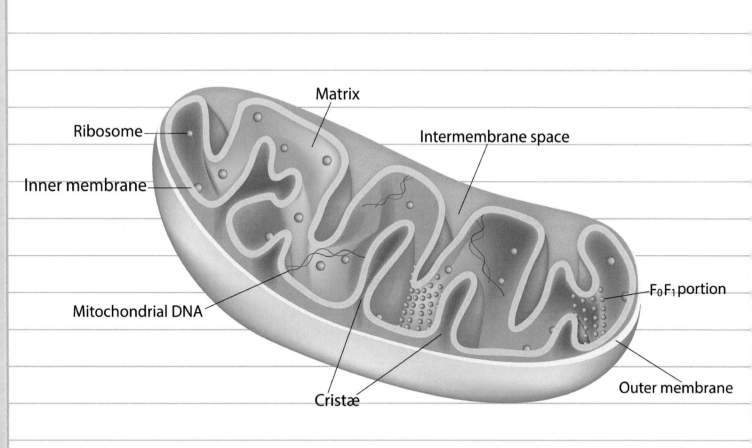

Matrix

Ribosome

Intermembrane space

Inner membrane

F_0F_1 portion

Mitochondrial DNA

Outer membrane

Cristæ

RIBOSOME

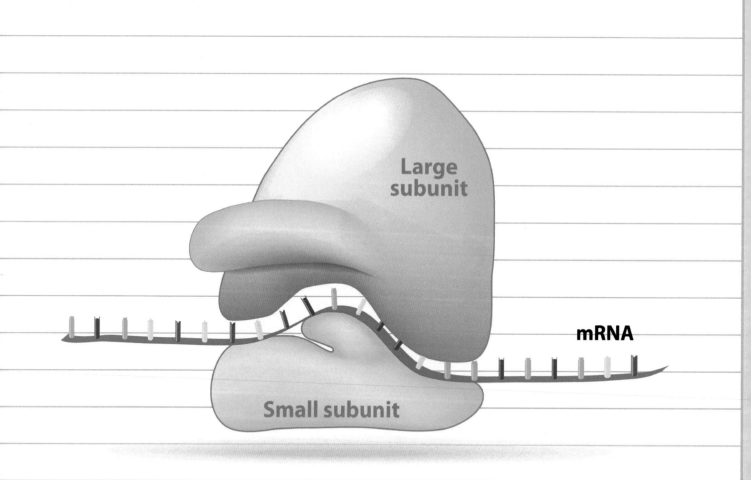

CHLOROPLAST

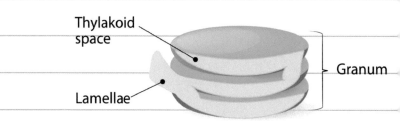

Thylakoid space

Lamellae

Granum

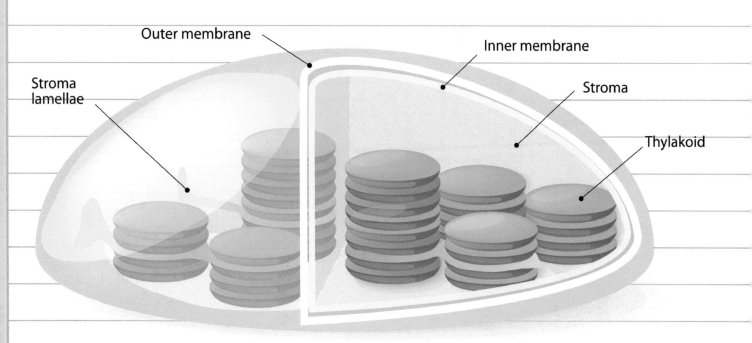

Outer membrane

Inner membrane

Stroma

Stroma lamellae

Thylakoid

OSMOSIS IN A PLANT CELL

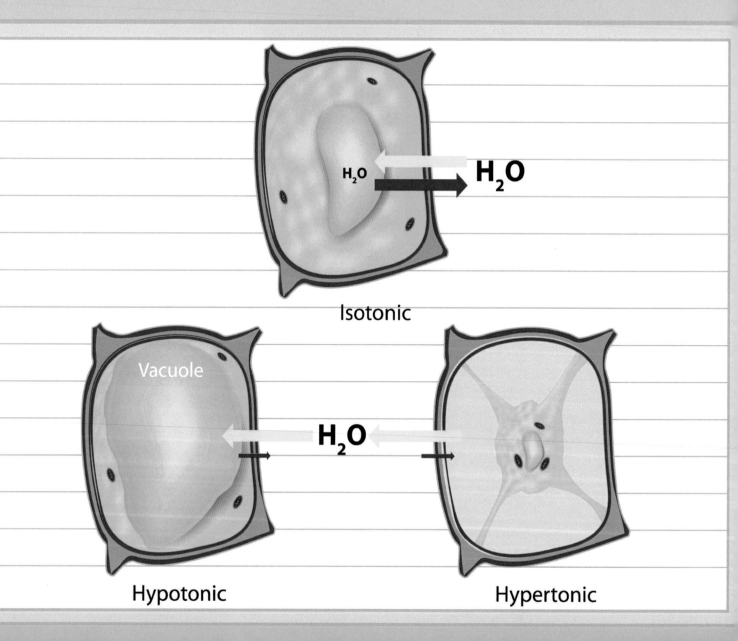

H_2O

H_2O

Isotonic

Vacuole

H_2O

Hypotonic

Hypertonic

FUNGI CELL

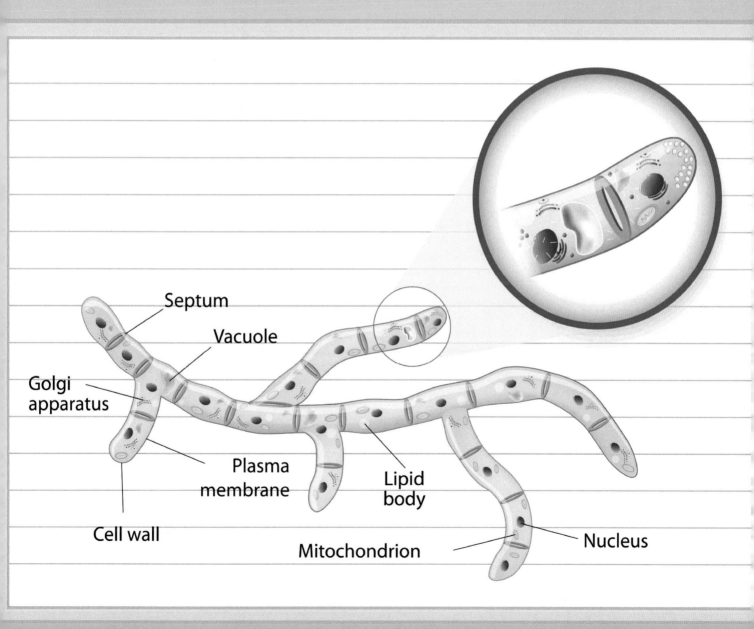

AUXIN

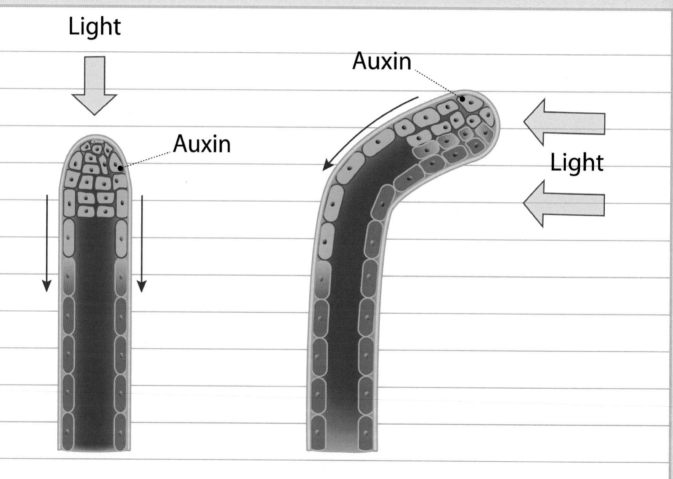

Light

Auxin

Auxin

Light

Auxin spreads equally down both sides of the plant

Auxin collects on the shady side

CENTRIOLE

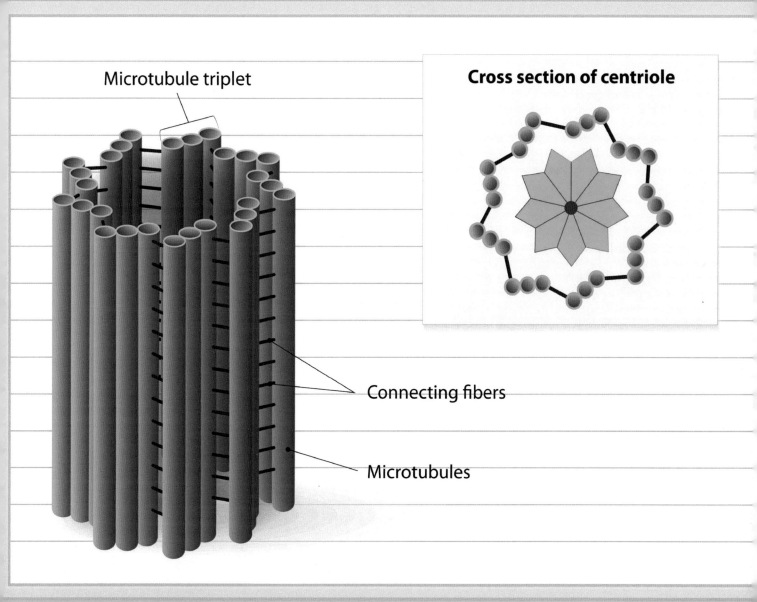

Microtubule triplet

Cross section of centriole

Connecting fibers

Microtubules

ANIMAL CELL

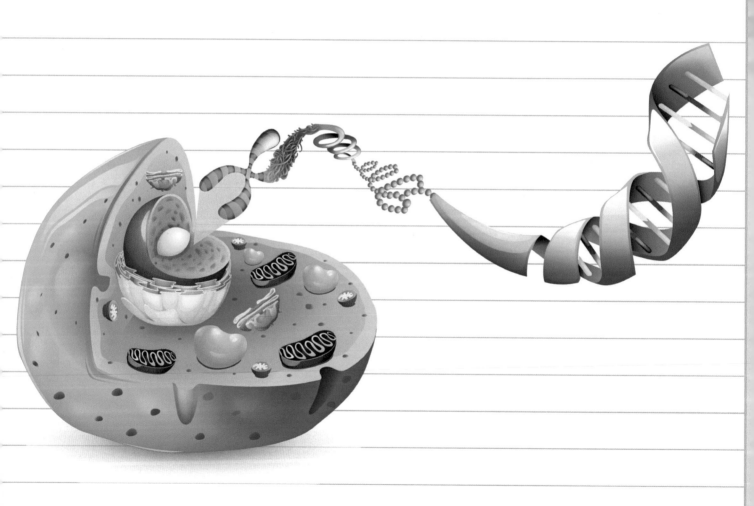

AND IT'S STRUCTURE

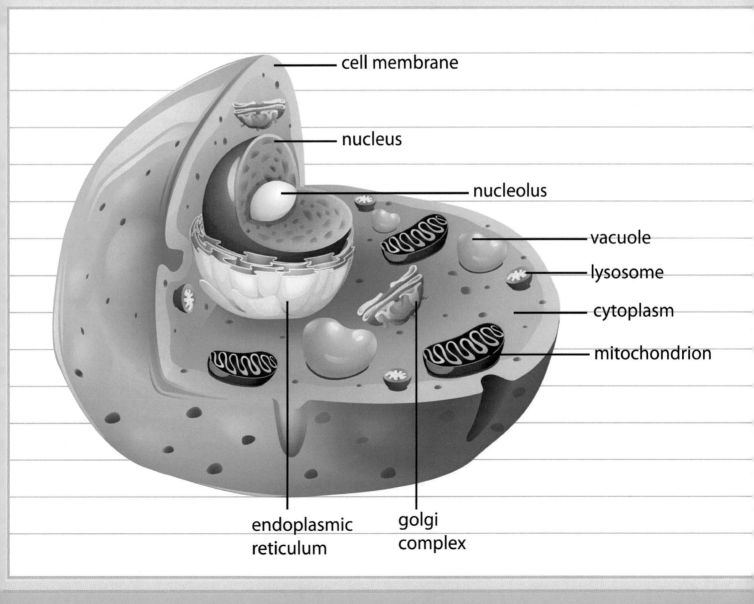

cell membrane

nucleus

nucleolus

vacuole

lysosome

cytoplasm

mitochondrion

endoplasmic reticulum

golgi complex

HUMAN CELLS

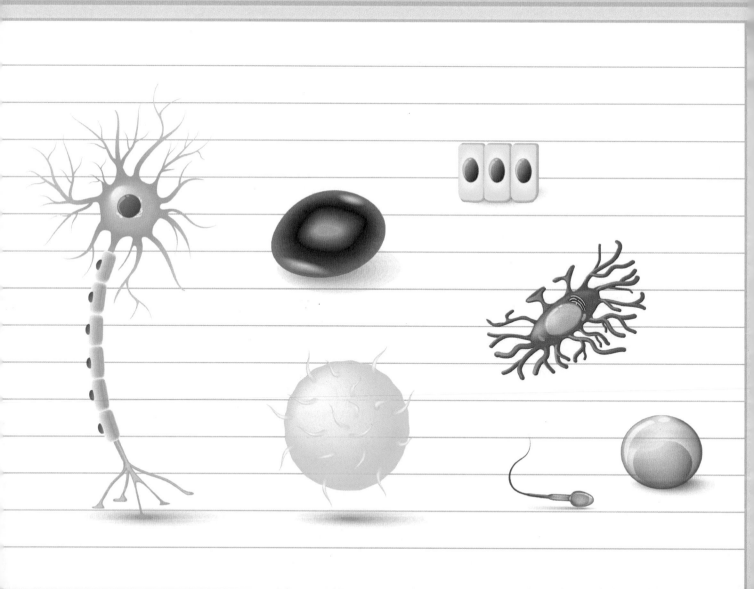

HUMAN NERVE CELLS

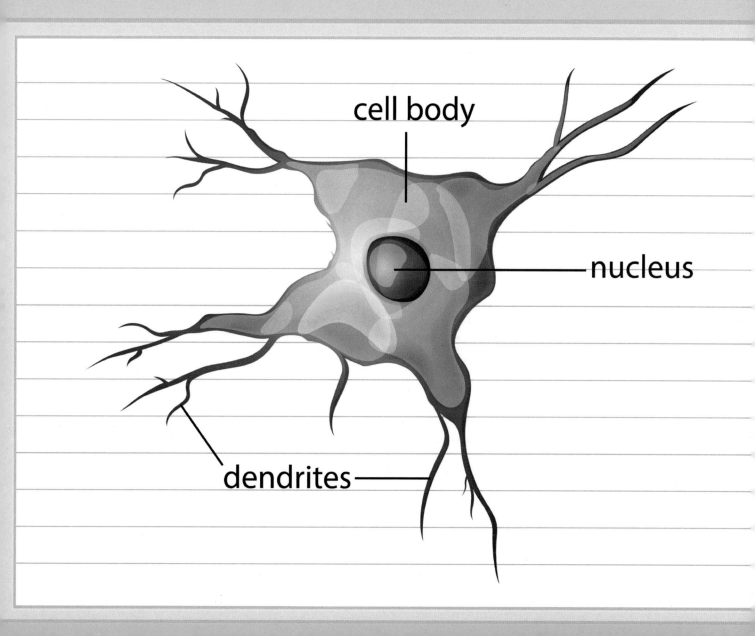

cell body

nucleus

dendrites

NEURONS AND NEUROGLIAL CELLS

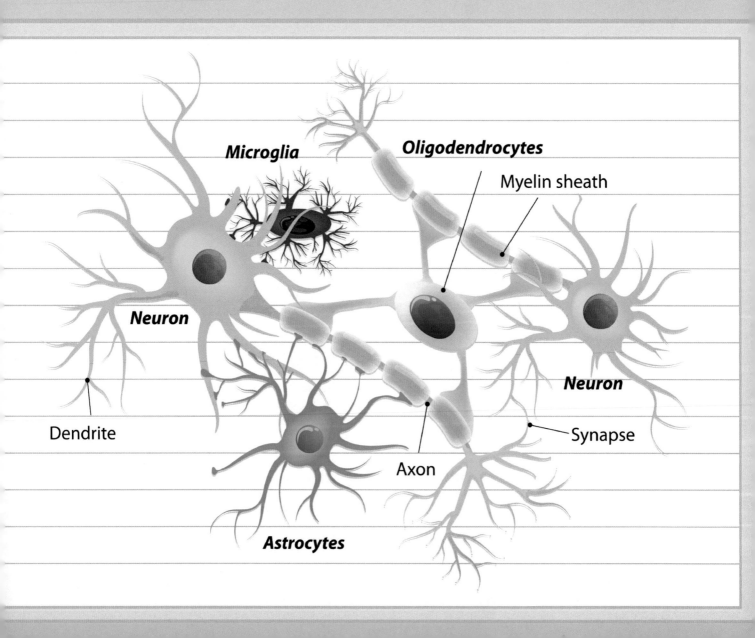

NEURON

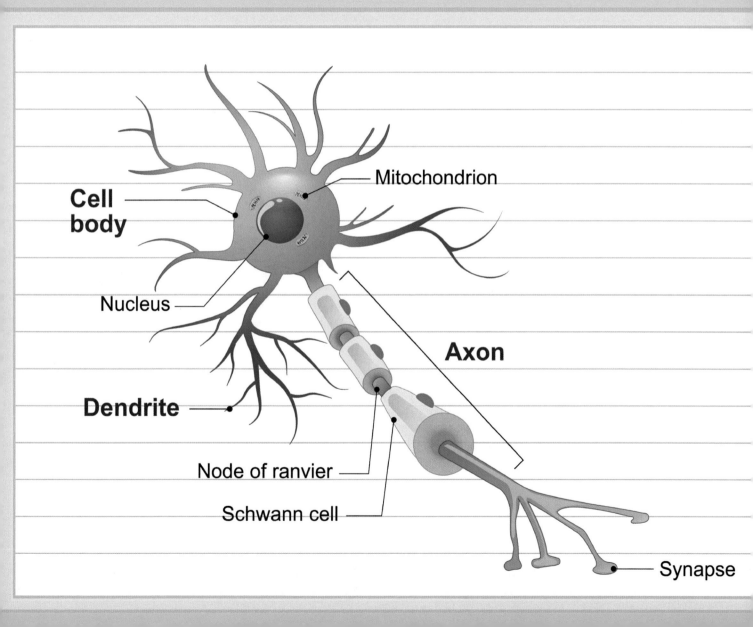

DEOXYRIBONUCLEIC ACID (DNA) STRUCTURE

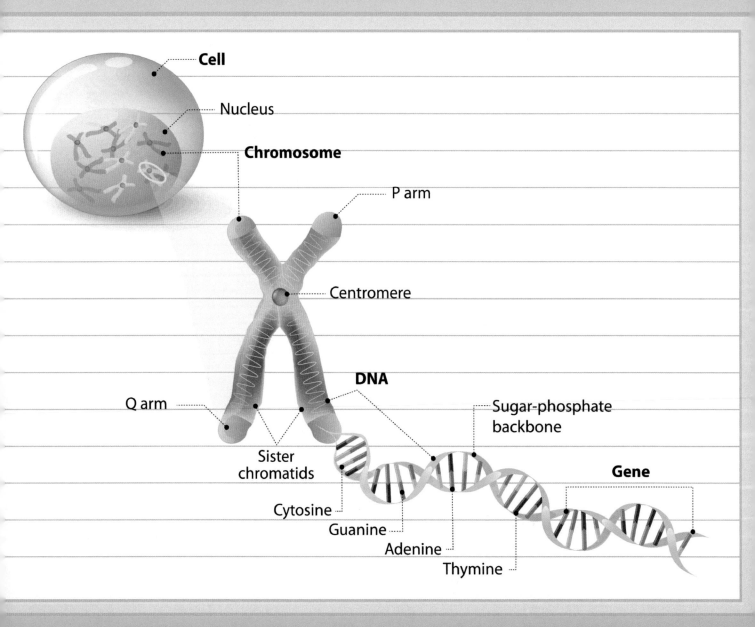

TELOMERE

A region of repetitive nucleotide sequences
at each end of a chromosome

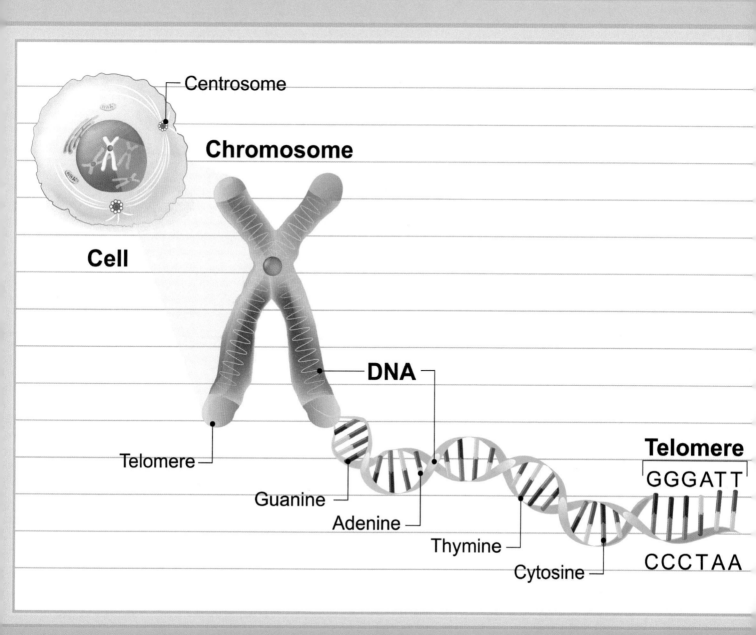

COMPONENTS OF BLOOD

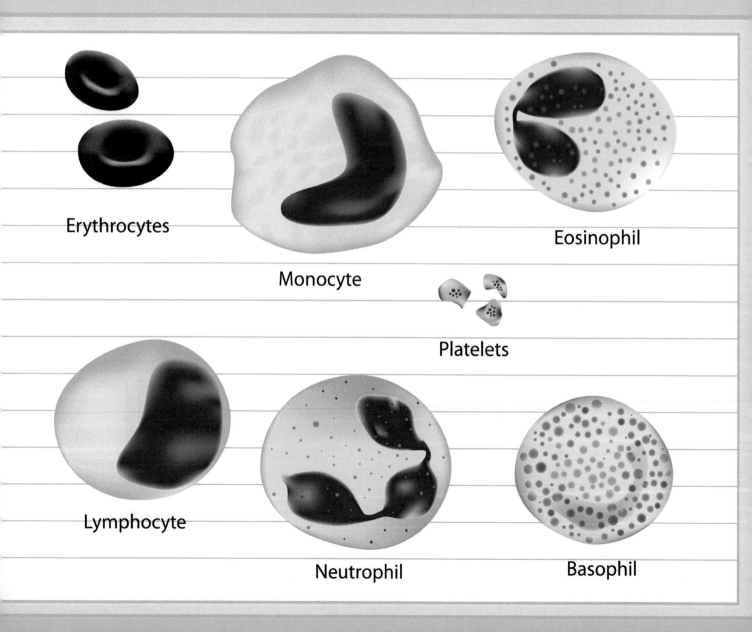

Erythrocytes

Monocyte

Eosinophil

Platelets

Lymphocyte

Neutrophil

Basophil

WHITE BLOOD CELLS

Lymphocyte

Basophil

Neutrophil

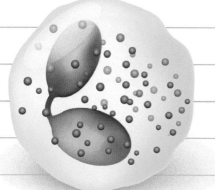

Eosinophil

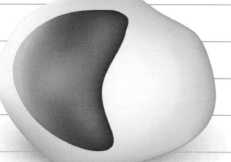

Monocyte

RED BLOOD CELL

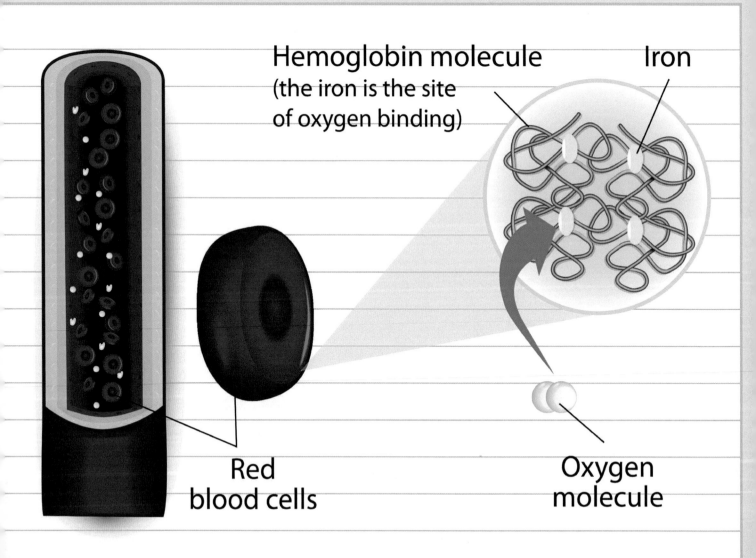

Hemoglobin molecule
(the iron is the site
of oxygen binding)

Iron

Red
blood cells

Oxygen
molecule

THE ELEMENTS OF BLOOD

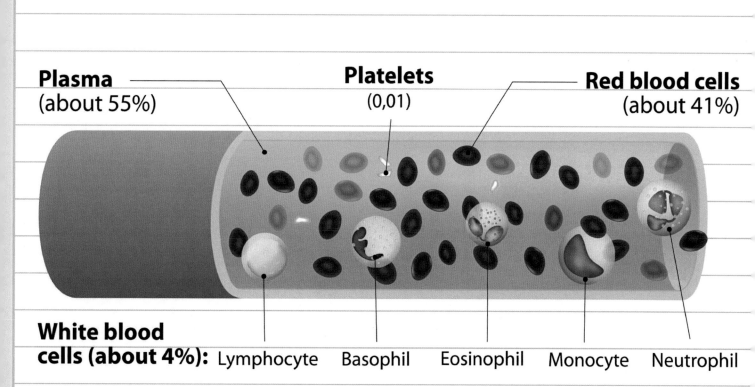

Plasma (about 55%)

Platelets (0,01)

Red blood cells (about 41%)

White blood cells (about 4%): Lymphocyte   Basophil   Eosinophil   Monocyte   Neutrophil

CELL MEMBRANE

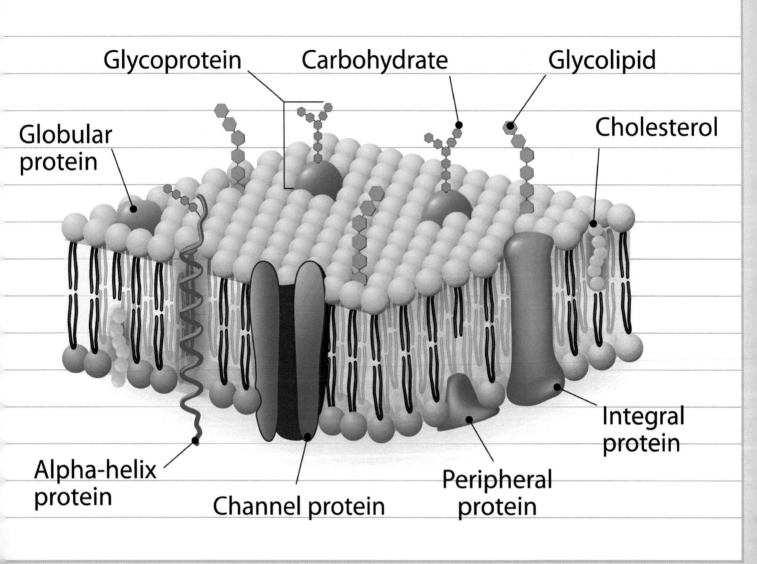

Glycoprotein

Carbohydrate

Glycolipid

Globular protein

Cholesterol

Alpha-helix protein

Channel protein

Peripheral protein

Integral protein

ANTIGEN-PRESENTING CELLS

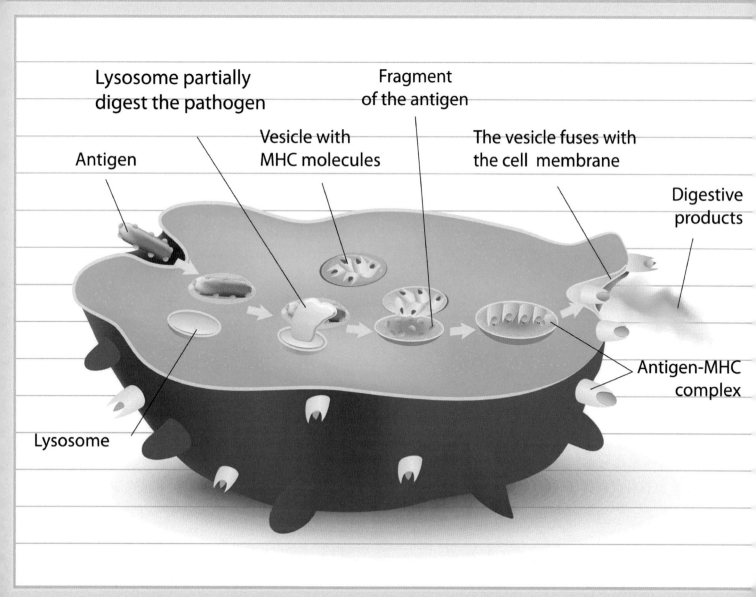

Lysosome partially digest the pathogen

Fragment of the antigen

Antigen

Vesicle with MHC molecules

The vesicle fuses with the cell membrane

Digestive products

Lysosome

Antigen-MHC complex

TYPES OF MUSCLE CELLS

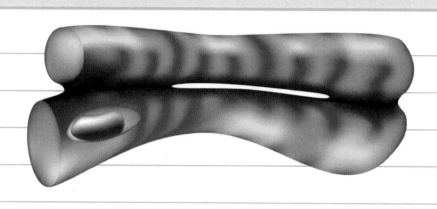

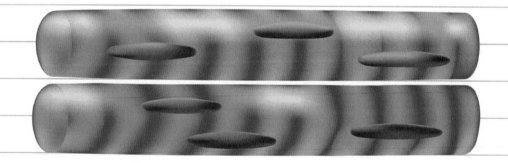

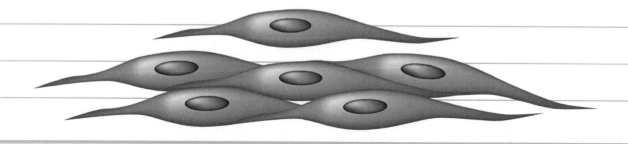

CARDIAC MUSCLE CELLS

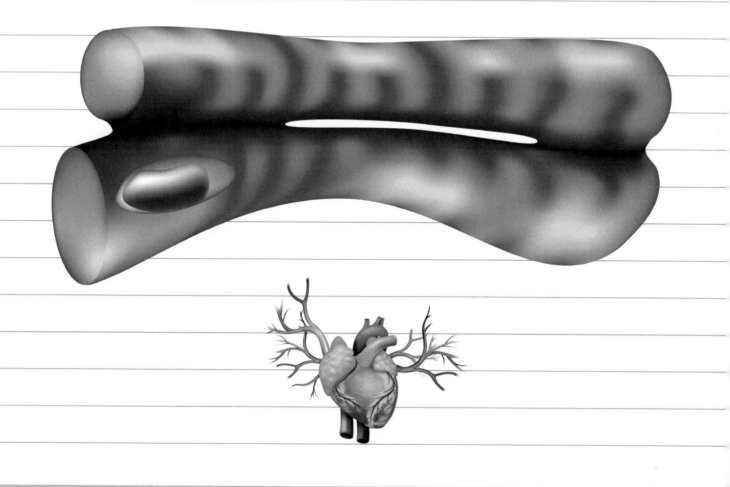

SKELETAL MUSCLE CELLS

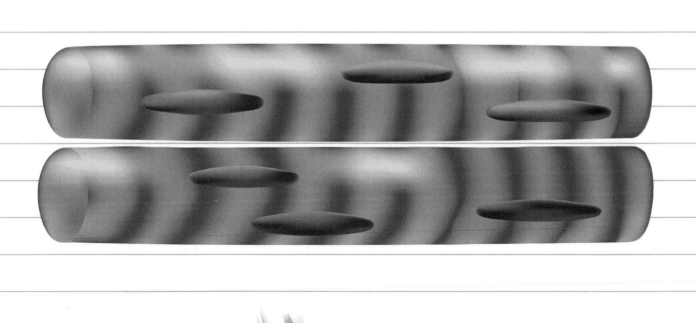

SMOOTH MUSCLE CELLS

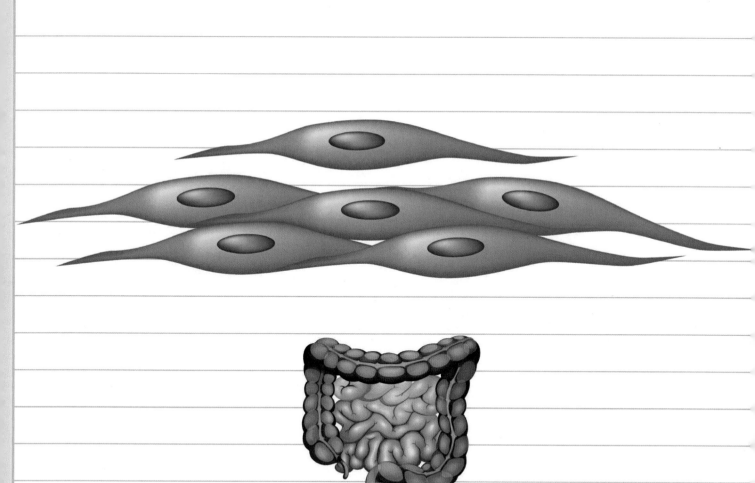

PHOTORECEPTOR CELLS

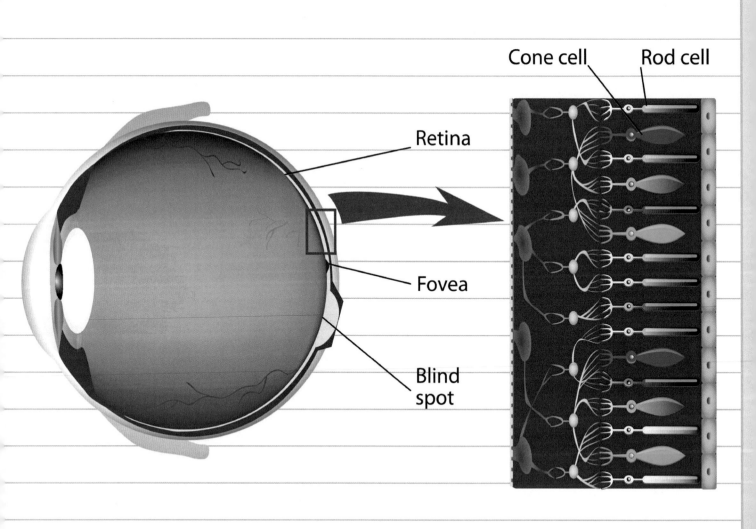

Cone cell   Rod cell

Retina

Fovea

Blind spot

FAT CELLS

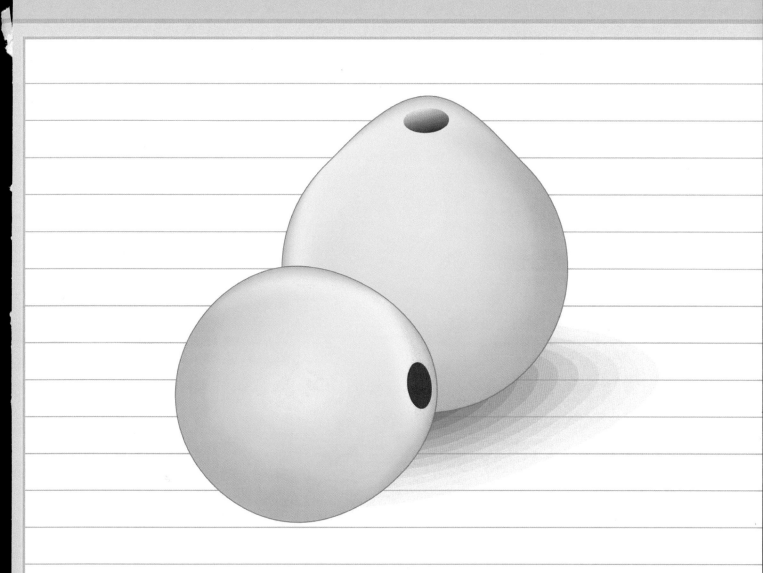

BONE CELL

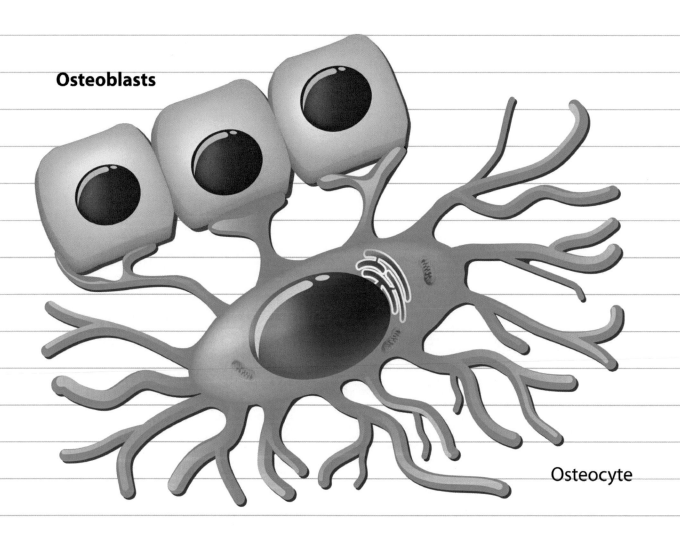

Osteoblasts

Osteocyte

INTESTINAL EPITHELIAL CELL

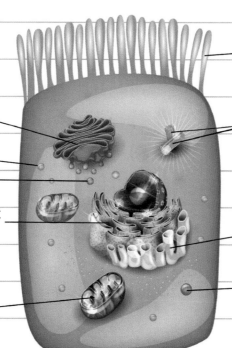

GOLGI COMPLEX

LISOSOME

VESICLE

ROUGH EDNOPLASMIC
RETICULUM

MITOCHONDRION

MICROVILLI

CENTRIOLES

SMOOTH EDNOPLASMIC
RETICULUM

PEROXISOME

LET US SEE WHAT YOU HAVE LEARNED ABOUT PLANT & ANIMAL CELLS

What is the name of this plant cell element?

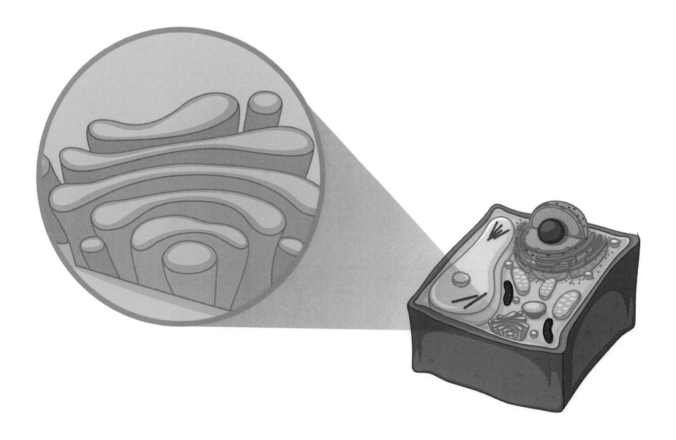

_____

write your answer here

What is the name of this plant cell element?

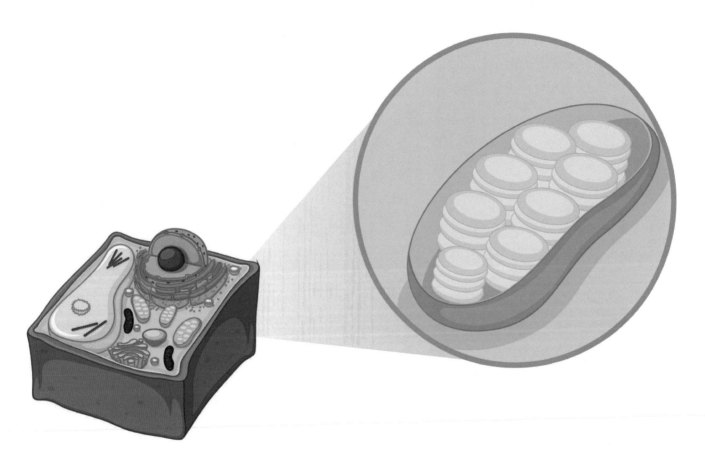

_____

write your answer here

What is the component name for this white blood cell?

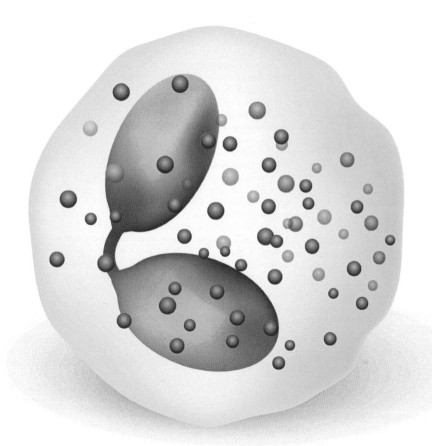

_____

write your answer here

What type of muscle cell is shown below?

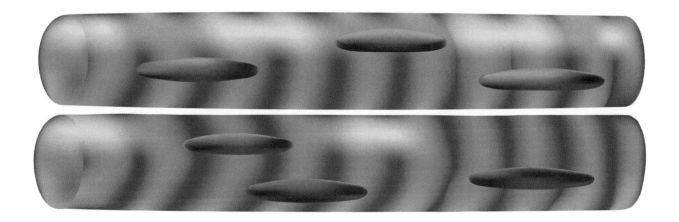

_____

write your answer here

This cell element is called...what?

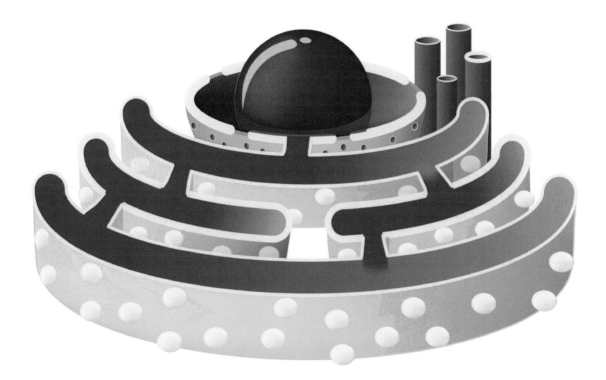

_____

write your answer here

ANSWERS

1. **Golgi Apparatus**

2. **Chloroplast**

3. **Eosinophil**

4. **Skeletal Muscle Cell**

5. **Endoplasmic Reticulum**

Visit

BABY PROFESSOR
EDUCATION KIDS

www.BabyProfessorBooks.com

to download Free Baby Professor eBooks
and view our catalog of new and exciting
Children's Books

Made in the USA
Columbia, SC
15 July 2020